50 Baroque Solos for Classical Guitar

Arranged by Mark Phillips

PLAYBACK+
Speed • Pitch • Balance • Loop

To access audio visit:
www.halleonard.com/mylibrary

8816-3701-1651-4844

ISBN 978-1-57560-740-5

HAL•LEONARD®

Copyright © 2004 Cherry Lane Music Company
International Copyright Secured   All Rights Reserved

For all works contained herein:
Unauthorized copying, arranging, adapting, recording, Internet posting, public performance,
or other distribution of the music in this publication is an infringement of copyright.
Infringers are liable under the law.

Visit Hal Leonard Online at
www.halleonard.com

Contact Us:
Hal Leonard
7777 West Bluemound Road
Milwaukee, WI 53213
Email: info@halleonard.com

In Europe contact:
Hal Leonard Europe Limited
42 Wigmore Street
Marylebone, London, W1U 2RN
Email: info@halleonardeurope.com

In Australia contact:
Hal Leonard Australia Pty. Ltd.
4 Lentara Court
Cheltenham, Victoria, 3192 Australia
Email: info@halleonard.com.au

Contents

Aria

Johann Sebastian Bach

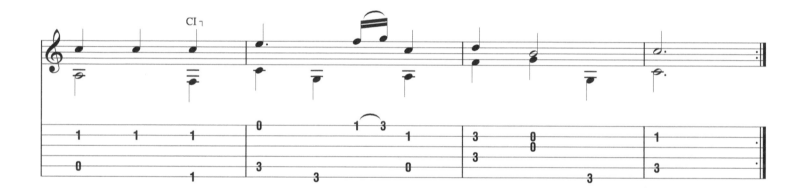

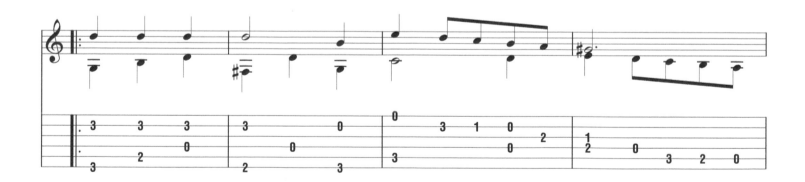

This Arrangement © 2004 Cherry Lane Music Company
International Copyright Secured   All Rights Reserved

Be Content

Johann Sebastian Bach

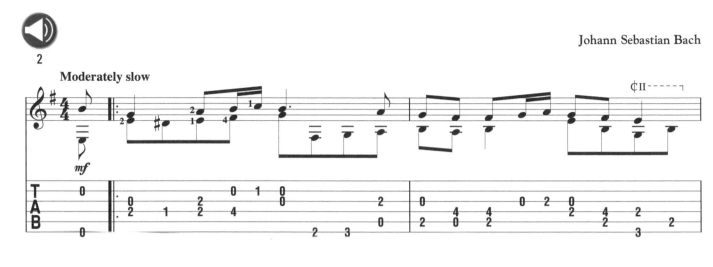

This Arrangement © 2004 Cherry Lane Music Company
International Copyright Secured   All Rights Reserved

Be Thou with Me

Johann Sebastian Bach

This Arrangement © 2004 Cherry Lane Music Company
International Copyright Secured   All Rights Reserved

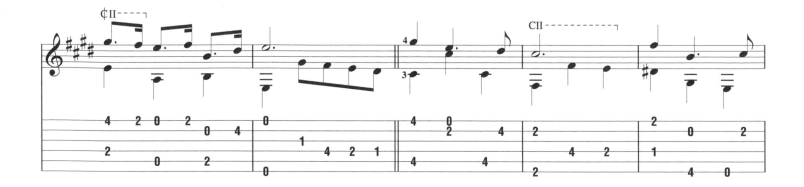

Gavotte
(from French Suite No. 5)

Johann Sebastian Bach

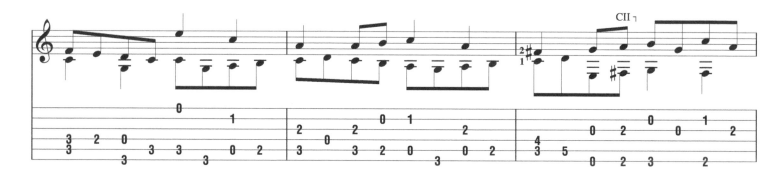

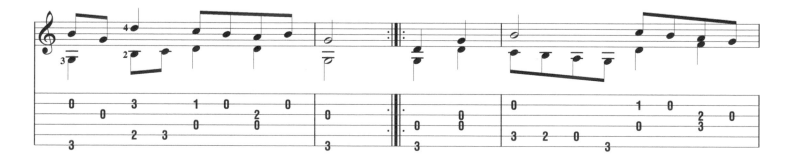

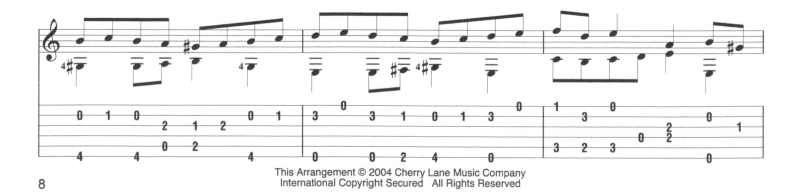

This Arrangement © 2004 Cherry Lane Music Company
International Copyright Secured   All Rights Reserved

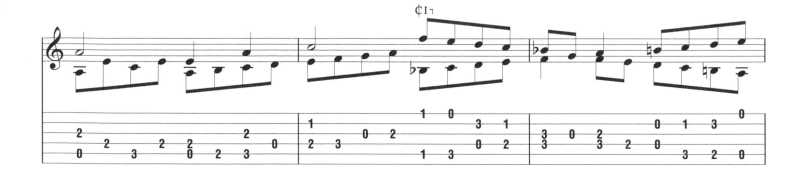

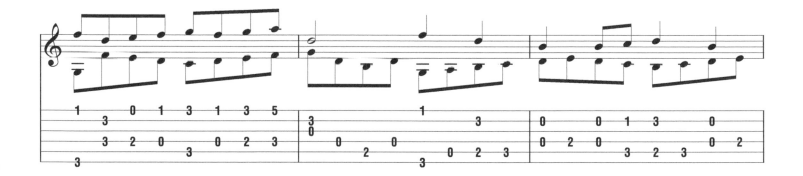

Sheep May Safely Graze

Johann Sebastian Bach

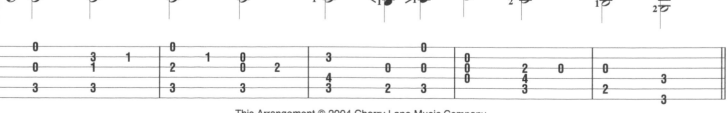

This Arrangement © 2004 Cherry Lane Music Company
International Copyright Secured   All Rights Reserved

Minuet 1

Johann Sebastian Bach

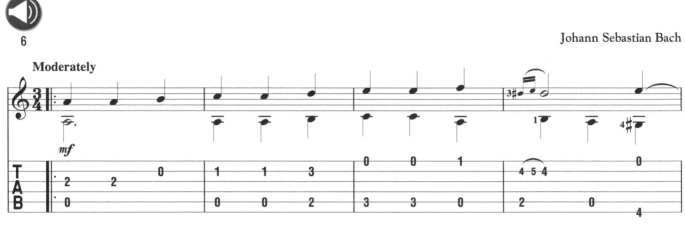

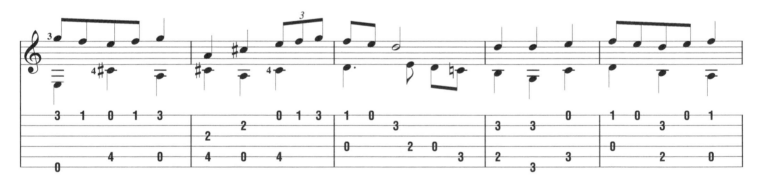

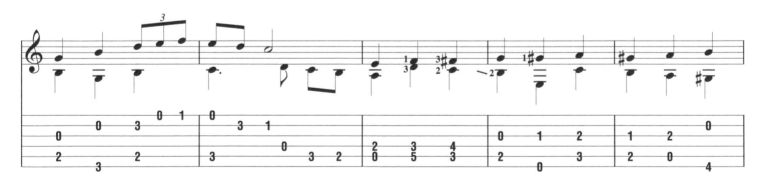

This Arrangement © 2004 Cherry Lane Music Company
International Copyright Secured   All Rights Reserved

Minuet 2

Johann Sebastian Bach

This Arrangement © 2004 Cherry Lane Music Company
International Copyright Secured   All Rights Reserved

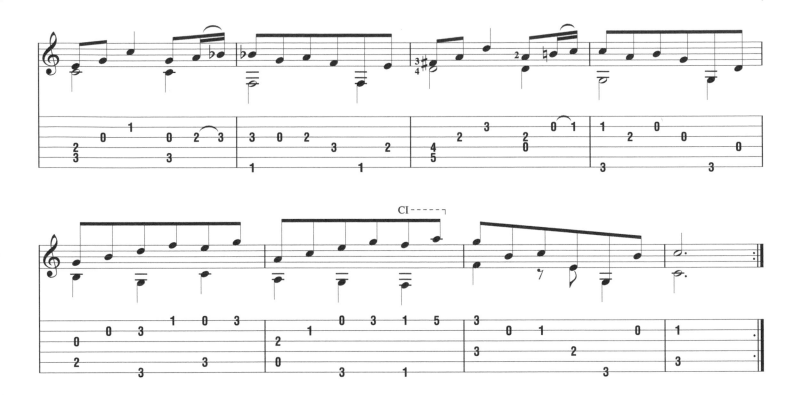

Sinfonia

(from Christmas Oratorio)

Johann Sebastian Bach

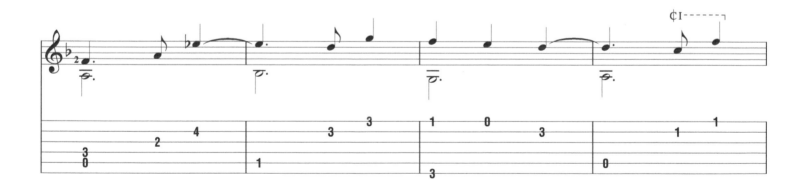

This Arrangement © 2004 Cherry Lane Music Company
International Copyright Secured   All Rights Reserved

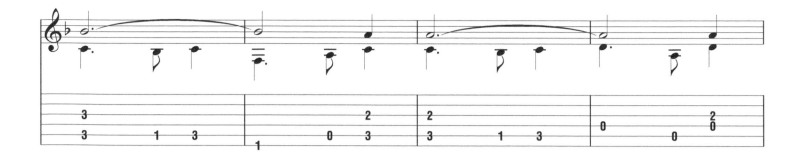

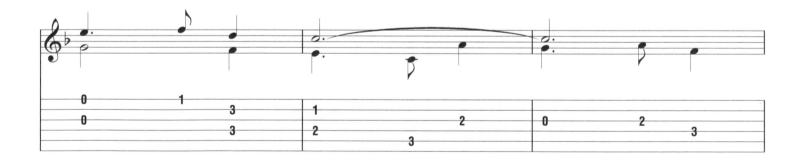

Air

John Blow

This Arrangement © 2004 Cherry Lane Music Company
International Copyright Secured   All Rights Reserved

Largo

Arcangelo Corelli

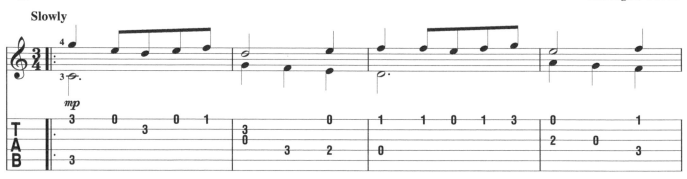

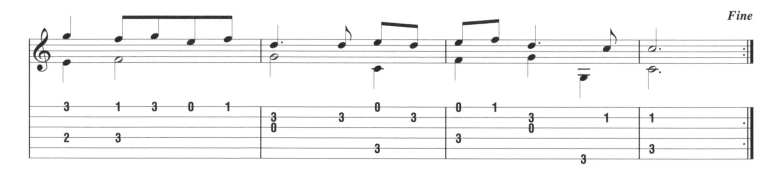

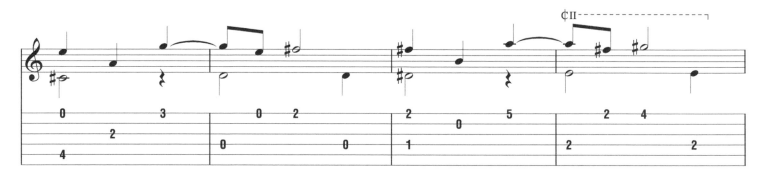

This Arrangement © 2004 Cherry Lane Music Company
International Copyright Secured   All Rights Reserved

Sarabande 1

Arcangelo Corelli

This Arrangement © 2004 Cherry Lane Music Company
International Copyright Secured   All Rights Reserved

Sarabande 2

Arcangelo Corelli

This Arrangement © 2004 Cherry Lane Music Company
International Copyright Secured   All Rights Reserved

Cuckoos
(from French Follies)

François Couperin

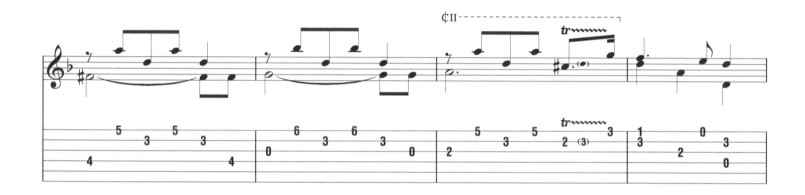

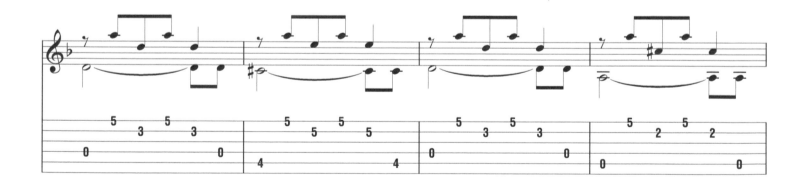

This Arrangement © 2004 Cherry Lane Music Company
International Copyright Secured   All Rights Reserved

The Harvesters

François Couperin

This Arrangement © 2004 Cherry Lane Music Company
International Copyright Secured   All Rights Reserved

Le Petit Rien

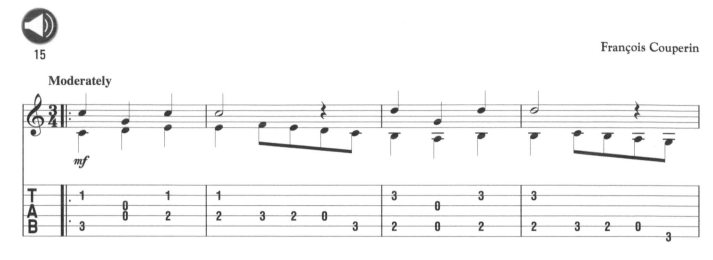

François Couperin

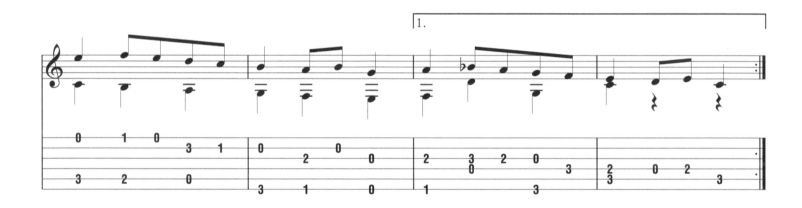

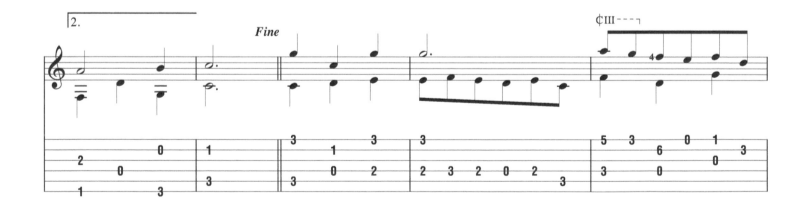

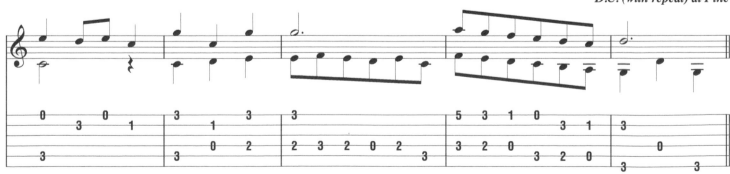

This Arrangement © 2004 Cherry Lane Music Company
International Copyright Secured   All Rights Reserved

The Thorny One

François Couperin

This Arrangement © 2004 Cherry Lane Music Company
International Copyright Secured   All Rights Reserved

Noël

Louis-Claude Daquin

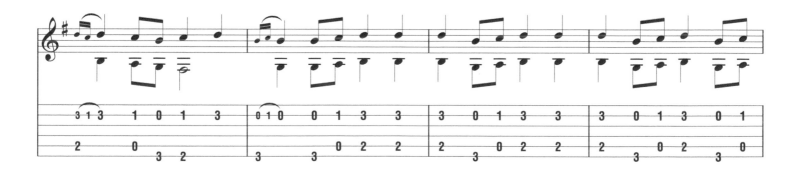

This Arrangement © 2004 Cherry Lane Music Company
International Copyright Secured   All Rights Reserved

Minuet

Elisabeth-Claude Jacquet de la Guerre

18

Moderately

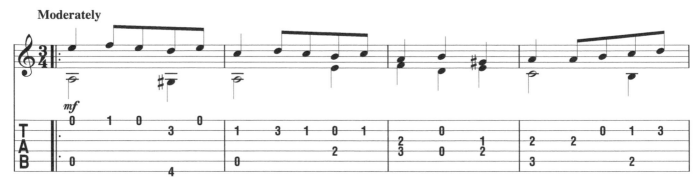

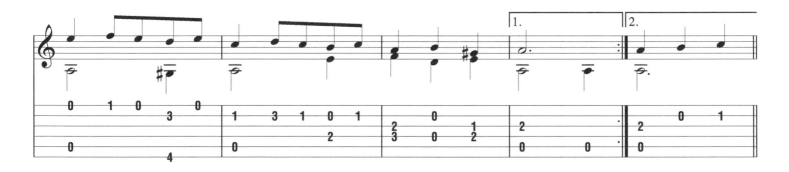

This Arrangement © 2004 Cherry Lane Music Company
International Copyright Secured   All Rights Reserved

Gavotte

Charles Dieupart

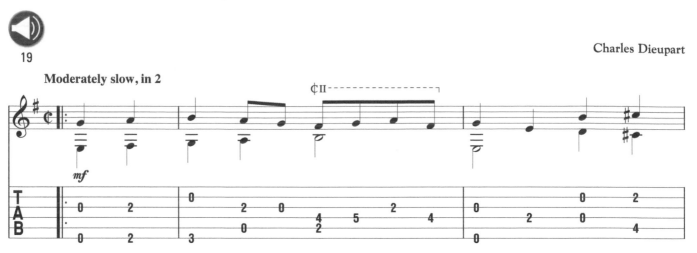

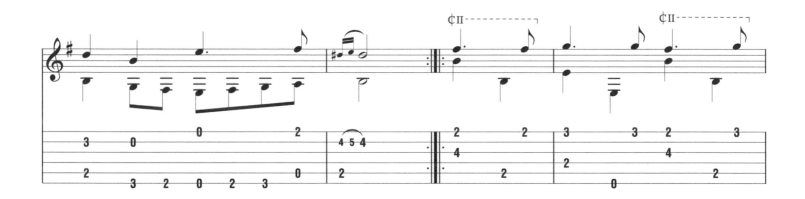

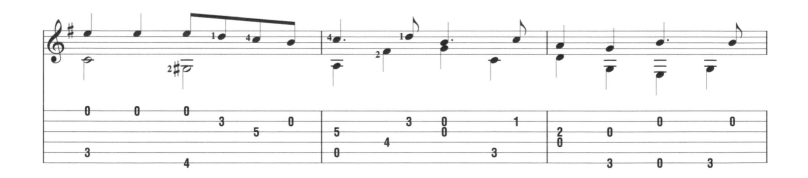

This Arrangement © 2004 Cherry Lane Music Company
International Copyright Secured   All Rights Reserved

Minuet

Charles Dieupart

Moderately

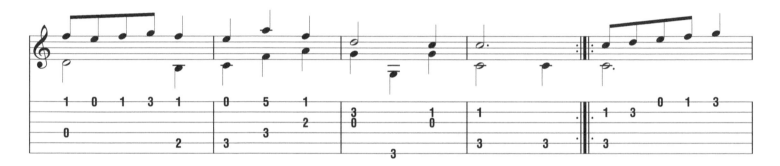

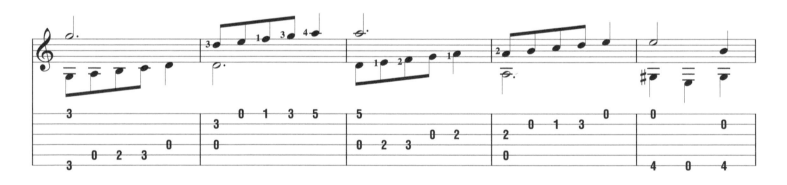

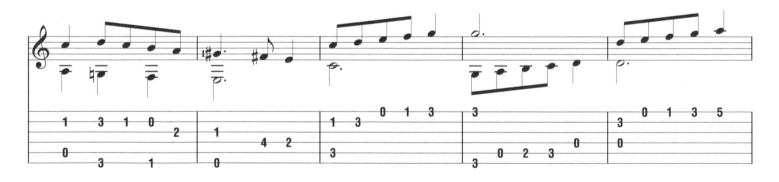

This Arrangement © 2004 Cherry Lane Music Company
International Copyright Secured   All Rights Reserved

Sonatina

William Duncombe

This Arrangement © 2004 Cherry Lane Music Company
International Copyright Secured   All Rights Reserved

Minuet

Adam Falckenhagen

This Arrangement © 2004 Cherry Lane Music Company
International Copyright Secured   All Rights Reserved

Air en Gavotte

Christopher Graupner

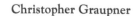

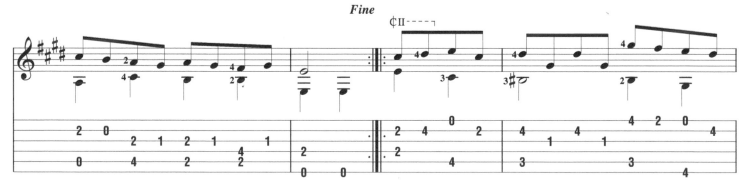

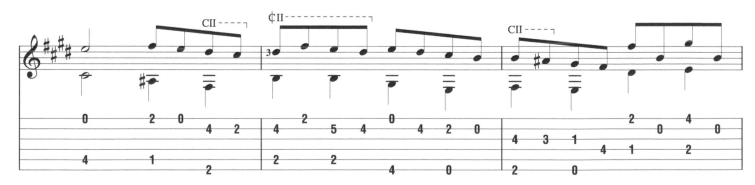

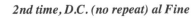

This Arrangement © 2004 Cherry Lane Music Company
International Copyright Secured   All Rights Reserved

Bourrée
(from Water Music Suite)

George Frederick Handel

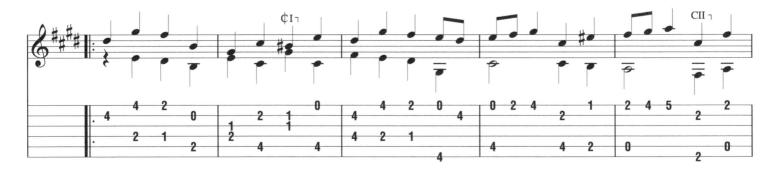

This Arrangement © 2004 Cherry Lane Music Company
International Copyright Secured   All Rights Reserved

Coro
(from Water Music Suite)

George Frederick Handel

25

This Arrangement © 2004 Cherry Lane Music Company
International Copyright Secured   All Rights Reserved

Gavotte

George Frederick Handel

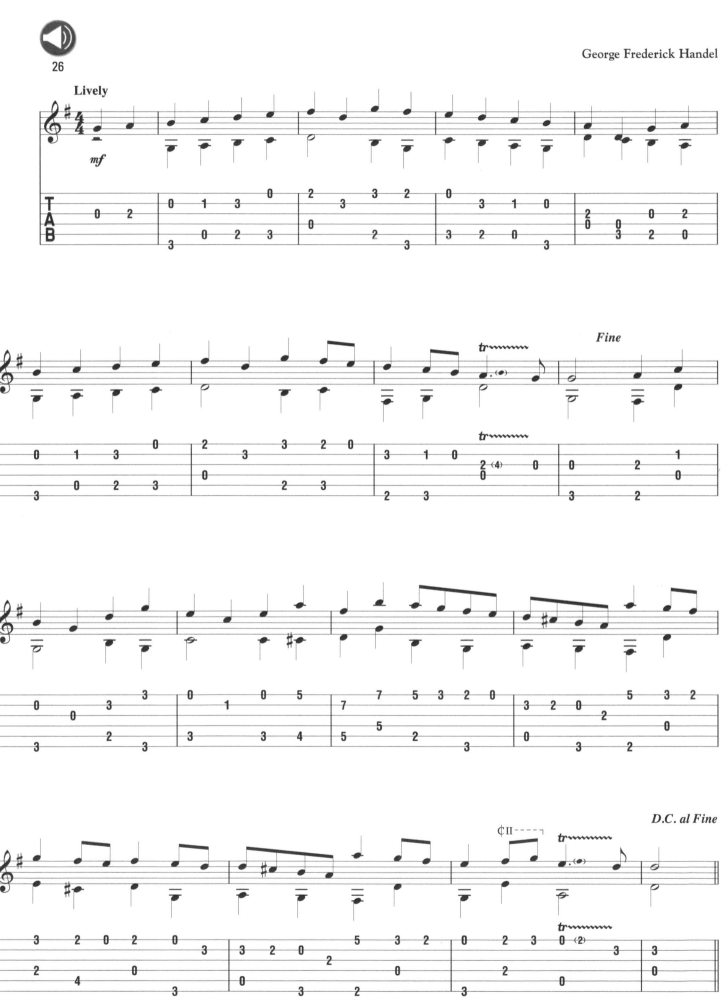

This Arrangement © 2004 Cherry Lane Music Company
International Copyright Secured   All Rights Reserved

March

(from Scipio)

George Frederick Handel

27

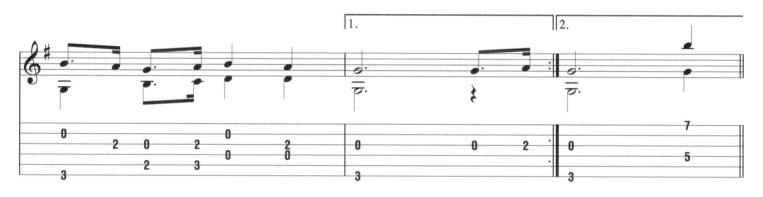

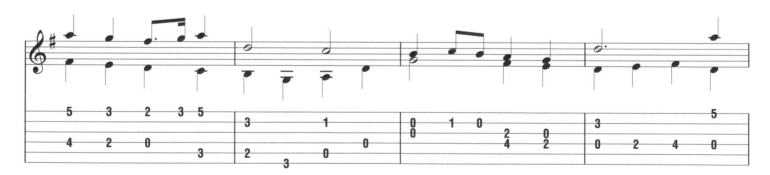

This Arrangement © 2004 Cherry Lane Music Company
International Copyright Secured   All Rights Reserved

Sarabande

George Frederick Handel

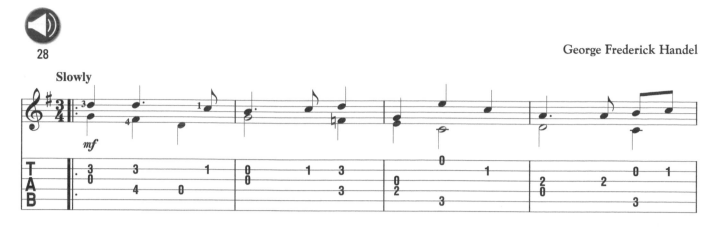

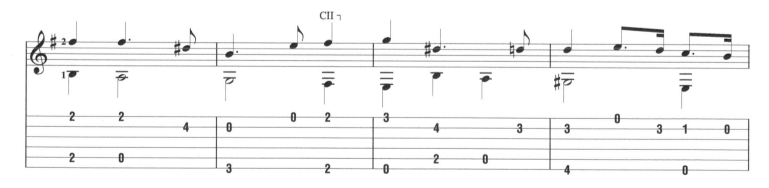

This Arrangement © 2004 Cherry Lane Music Company
International Copyright Secured   All Rights Reserved

Minuet 1

George Frederick Handel

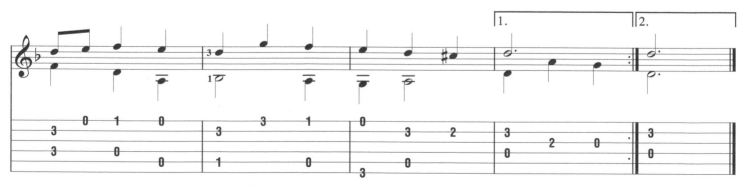

This Arrangement © 2004 Cherry Lane Music Company
International Copyright Secured   All Rights Reserved

Minuet 2

George Frederick Handel

This Arrangement © 2004 Cherry Lane Music Company
International Copyright Secured   All Rights Reserved

Minuet 3

George Frederick Handel

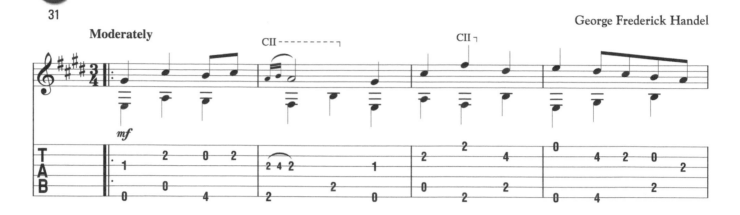

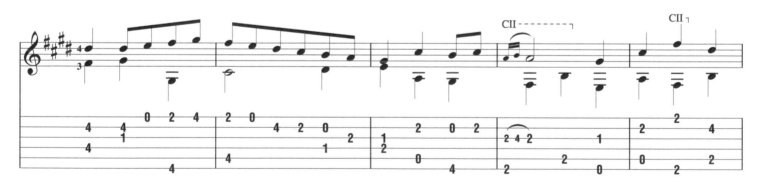

This Arrangement © 2004 Cherry Lane Music Company
International Copyright Secured   All Rights Reserved

Passepied 1

George Frederick Handel

This Arrangement © 2004 Cherry Lane Music Company
International Copyright Secured   All Rights Reserved

Passepied 2

George Frederick Handel

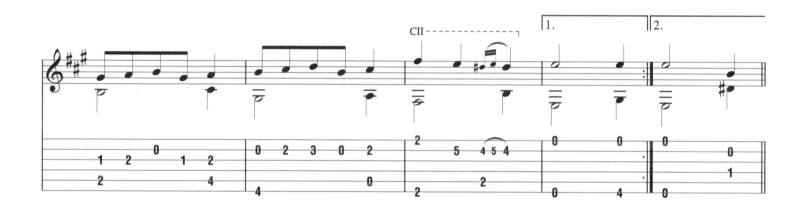

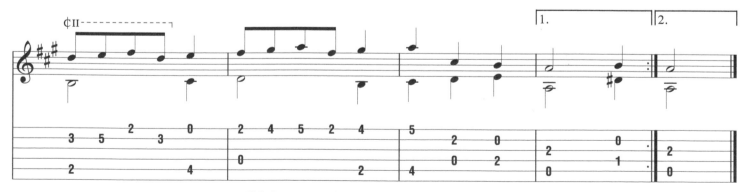

This Arrangement © 2004 Cherry Lane Music Company
International Copyright Secured   All Rights Reserved

Air

Henry Purcell

This Arrangement © 2004 Cherry Lane Music Company
International Copyright Secured   All Rights Reserved

A Farewell
(The Queen's Dolour)

Henry Purcell

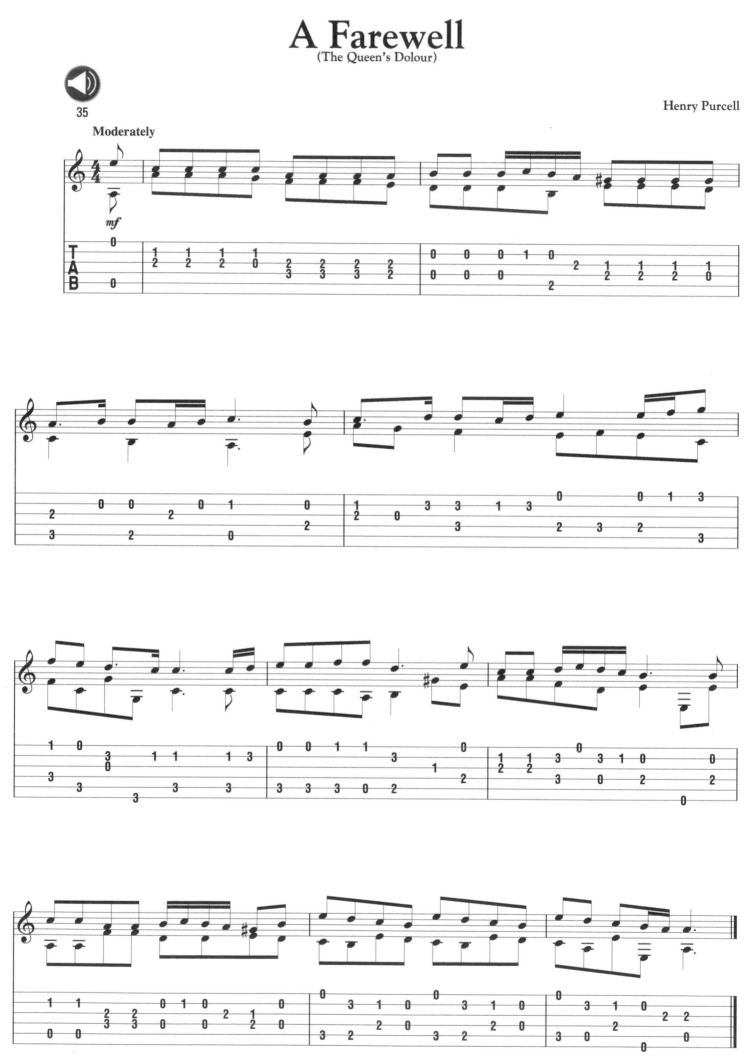

This Arrangement © 2004 Cherry Lane Music Company
International Copyright Secured   All Rights Reserved

Minuet

Henry Purcell

This Arrangement © 2004 Cherry Lane Music Company
International Copyright Secured   All Rights Reserved

Rigadoon

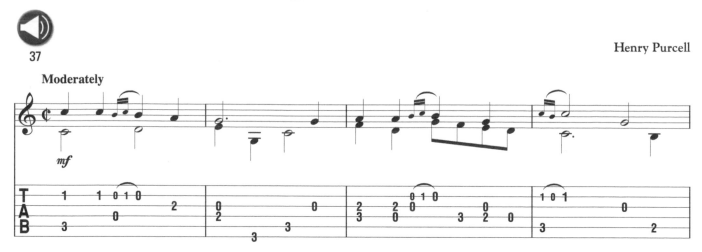

Henry Purcell

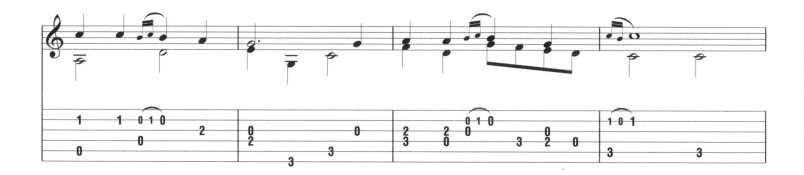

This Arrangement © 2004 Cherry Lane Music Company
International Copyright Secured   All Rights Reserved

Rigaudon

Jean-Phillippe Rameau

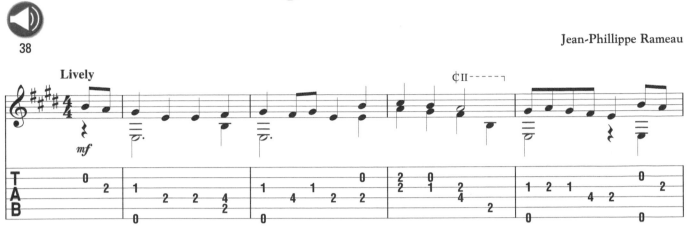

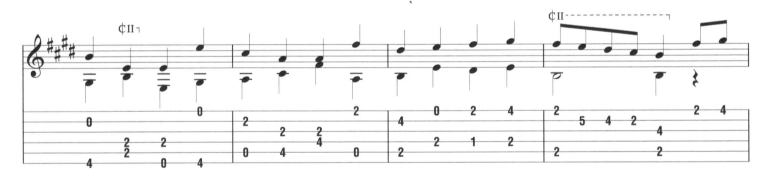

This Arrangement © 2004 Cherry Lane Music Company
International Copyright Secured   All Rights Reserved

Rondino

Jean Philippe Rameau

This Arrangement © 2004 Cherry Lane Music Company
International Copyright Secured   All Rights Reserved

Dance Song

This Arrangement © 2004 Cherry Lane Music Company
International Copyright Secured   All Rights Reserved

Musical Pastime

Valentin Rathgeber

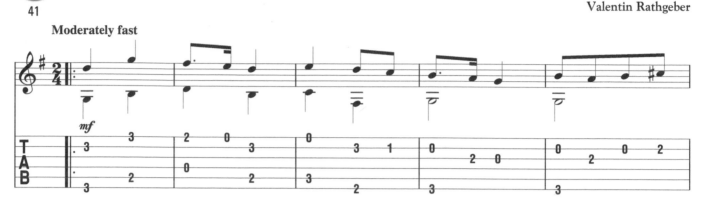

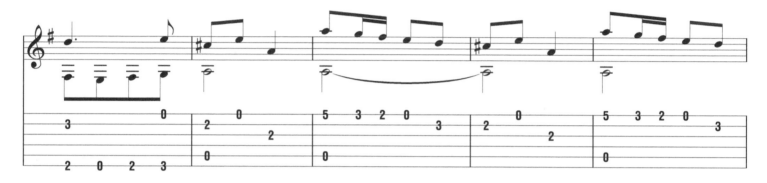

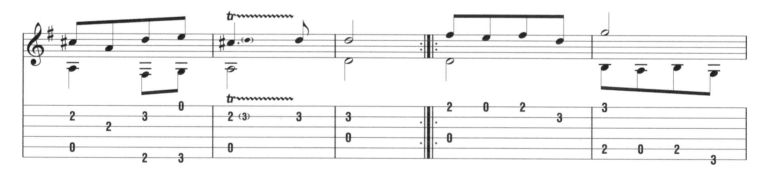

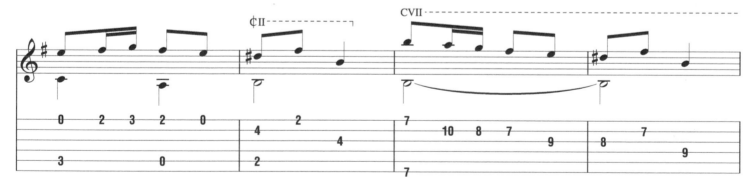

This Arrangement © 2004 Cherry Lane Music Company
International Copyright Secured   All Rights Reserved

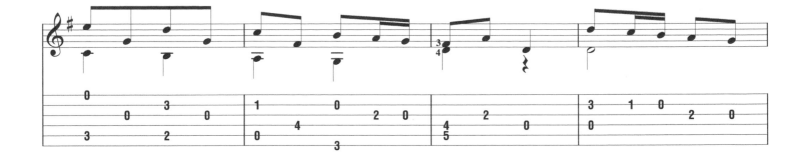

Larghetto

42

Domenico Scarlatti

Moderately slow

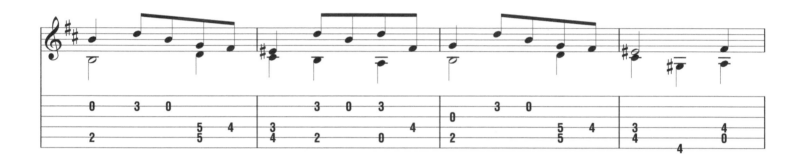

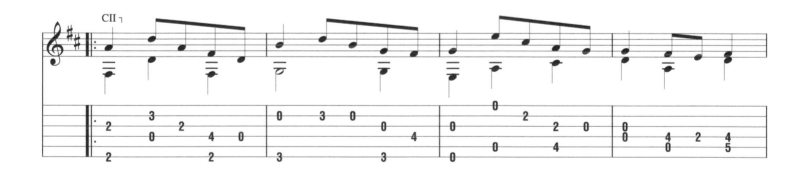

This Arrangement © 2004 Cherry Lane Music Company
International Copyright Secured   All Rights Reserved

Minuet 1

Domenico Scarlatti

This Arrangement © 2004 Cherry Lane Music Company
International Copyright Secured   All Rights Reserved

Minuet 2

Domenico Scarlatti

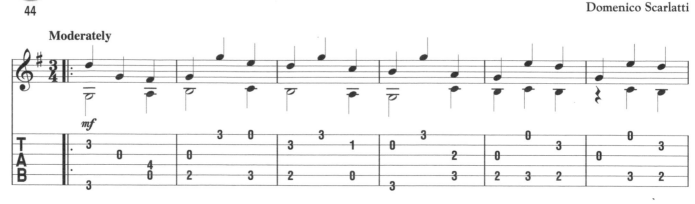

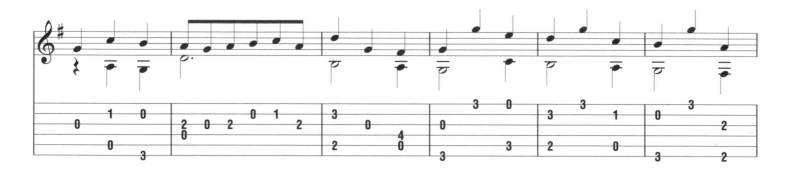

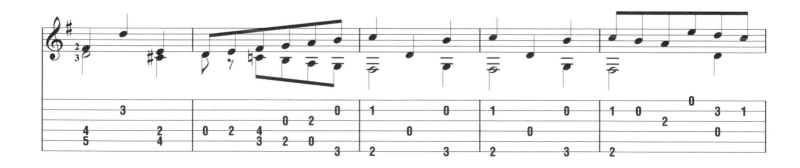

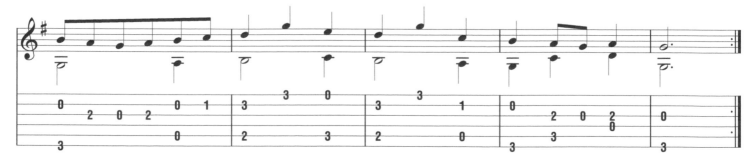

This Arrangement © 2004 Cherry Lane Music Company
International Copyright Secured   All Rights Reserved

Gigue

Domenico Scarlatti

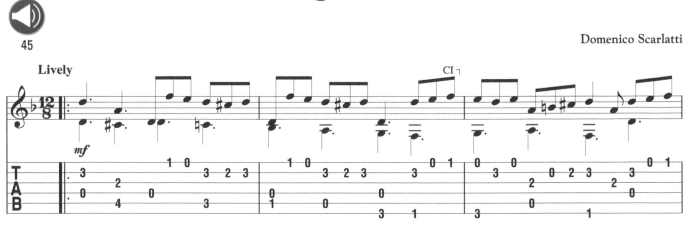

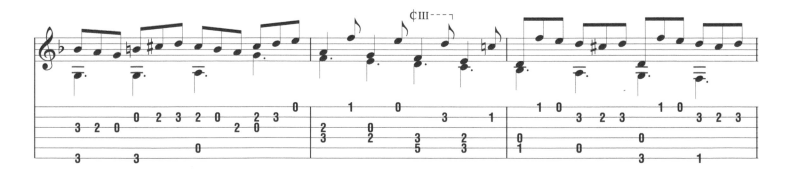

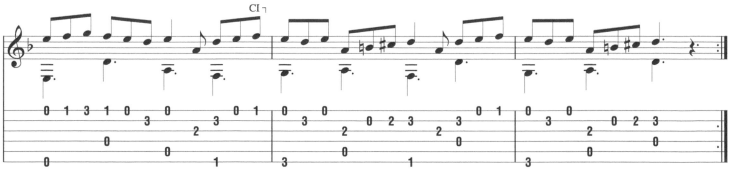

This Arrangement © 2004 Cherry Lane Music Company
International Copyright Secured   All Rights Reserved

Bourrée

Georg Philipp Telemann

This Arrangement © 2004 Cherry Lane Music Company
International Copyright Secured   All Rights Reserved

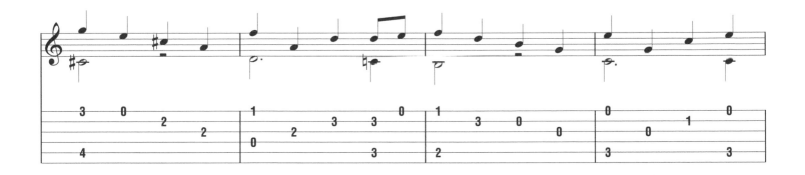

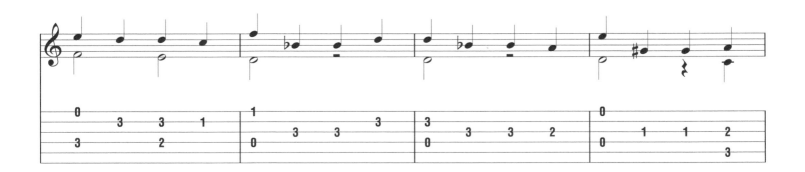

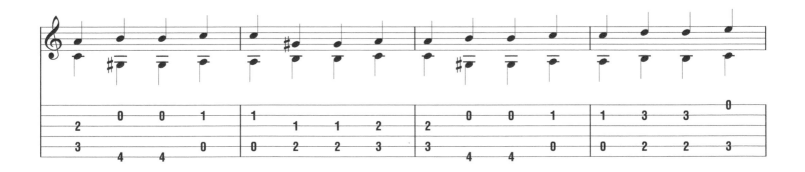

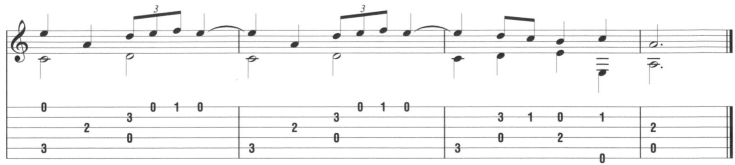

Burlesca

Georg Philipp Telemann

This Arrangement © 2004 Cherry Lane Music Company
International Copyright Secured   All Rights Reserved

Minuet

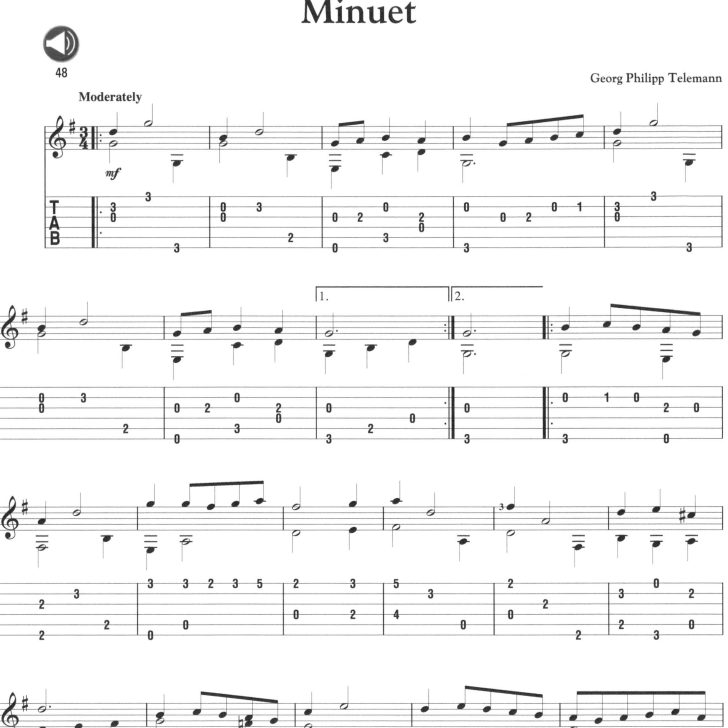

Georg Philipp Telemann

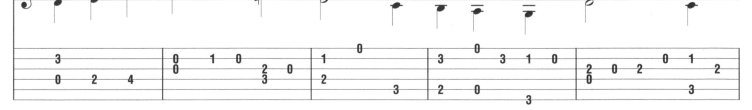

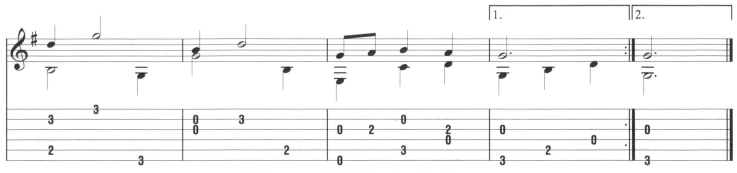

This Arrangement © 2004 Cherry Lane Music Company
International Copyright Secured   All Rights Reserved

Scherzino

Georg Phillip Telemann

This Arrangement © 2004 Cherry Lane Music Company
International Copyright Secured   All Rights Reserved

Minuet

Welzel von Radolt

This Arrangement © 2004 Cherry Lane Music Company
International Copyright Secured   All Rights Reserved

CLASSICAL GUITAR

INSTRUCTIONAL BOOKS & METHODS AVAILABLE FROM HAL LEONARD

CLASSICAL STUDIES FOR PICK-STYLE GUITAR

by William Leavitt
Berklee Press

This Berklee Workshop, featuring over 20 solos and duets by Bach, Carcassi, Paganini, Sor and other renowned composers, is designed to acquaint intermediate to advanced pick-style guitarists with some of the excellent classical music that is adaptable to pick-style guitar. With study and practice, this workshop will increase a player's knowledge and proficiency on this formidable instrument.
50449440................................$12.99

ÉTUDES SIMPLES FOR GUITAR

by Leo Brouwer
Editions Max Eschig

This new, completely revised and updated edition includes critical commentary and performance notes. Each study is accompanied by an introduction that illustrates its principal musical features and technical objectives, complete with suggestions and preparatory exercises.
50565810 Book/CD Pack........$26.99

FIRST BOOK FOR THE GUITAR

by Frederick Noad
G. Schirmer, Inc.

A beginner's manual to the classical guitar. Uses a systematic approach using the interesting solo and duet music written by Noad, one of the world's foremost guitar educators. No musical knowledge is necessary. Student can progress by simple stages. Many of the exercises are designed for a teacher to play with the students. Will increase student's enthusiasm, therefore increasing the desire to take lessons.
50334370 Part 1....................$12.99
50334520 Part 2....................$17.99
50335160 Part 3....................$16.99
50336760 Complete Edition.....................$32.99

HAL LEONARD CLASSICAL GUITAR METHOD

by Paul Henry

This comprehensive and easy-to-use beginner's guide uses the music of the master composers to teach you the basics of the classical style and technique. Includes pieces by Beethoven, Bach, Mozart, Schumann, Giuliani, Carcassi, Bathioli, Aguado, Tarrega, Purcell, and more. Includes all the basics plus info on PIMA technique, two- and three-part music, time signatures, key signatures, articulation, free stroke, rest stroke, composers, and much more.
00697376 Book/Online Audio (no tab)................$16.99
00142652 Book/Online Audio (with tab).............$17.99

A MODERN APPROACH TO CLASSICAL GUITAR

by Charles Duncan

This multi-volume method was developed to allow students to study the art of classical guitar within a new, more contemporary framework. For private, class or self-instruction.

00695114 Book 1 – Book Only.............................$8.99
00695113 Book 1 – Book/Online Audio................$12.99
00699204 Book 1 – Repertoire Book Only............$11.99
00699205 Book 1 – Repertoire Book/Online Audio . $16.99
00695116 Book 2 – Book Only.............................$7.99
00695115 Book 2 – Book/Online Audio................$12.99
00699208 Book 2 – Repertoire............................$12.99
00699202 Book 3 – Book Only.............................$9.99
00695117 Book 3 – Book/Online Audio................$14.99
00695119 Composite Book/CD Pack....................$32.99

100 GRADED CLASSICAL GUITAR STUDIES

Selected and Graded by Frederick Noad

Frederick Noad has selected 100 studies from the works of three outstanding composers of the classical period: Sor, Giuliani, and Carcassi. All these studies are invaluable for developing both right hand and left hand skills. Students and teachers will find this book invaluable for making technical progress. In addition, they will build a repertoire of some of the most melodious music ever written for the guitar.
14023154................................$29.99

CHRISTOPHER PARKENING GUITAR METHOD

THE ART & TECHNIQUE OF THE CLASSICAL GUITAR

Guitarists will learn basic classical technique by playing over 50 beautiful classical pieces, 26 exercises and 14 duets, and through numerous photos and illustrations. The method covers: rudiments of classical technique, note reading and music theory, selection and care of guitars, strategies for effective practicing, and much more!
00696023 Book 1/Online Audio $22.99
00695228 Book 1 (No Audio) $14.99
00696024 Book 2/Online Audio $22.99
00695229 Book 2 (No Audio) $14.99

SOLO GUITAR PLAYING

by Frederick M. Noad

Solo Guitar Playing can teach even the person with no previous musical training how to progress from simple single-line melodies to mastery of the guitar as a solo instrument. Fully illustrated with diagrams, photographs, and over 200 musical exercises and repertoire selections, these books offer instruction in every phase of classical guitar playing.
14023147 Book 1/Online Audio $34.99
14023153 Book 1 (Book Only) $24.99
14023151 Book 2 (Book Only) $19.99

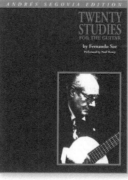

TWENTY STUDIES FOR THE GUITAR

ANDRÉS SEGOVIA EDITION

by Fernando Sor
Performed by Paul Henry

20 studies for the classical guitar written by Beethoven's contemporary, Fernando Sor, revised, edited and fingered by the great classical guitarist Andres Segovia. These essential repertoire pieces continue to be used by teachers and students to build solid classical technique. Features 50-minute demonstration audio.
00695012 Book/Online Audio $22.99
00006363 Book Only...$9.99

HAL•LEONARD®

Order these and more publications
from your favorite music retailer at
halleonard.com

Prices, contents and availability subject to change without notice.